BJ's Adventures In the Neighborhood

Author: Tomiko Cobb **Illustrator: Ika Wahyu**

Copyright © 2022 by Tomiko Cobb
All rights reserved. No part of this publication may be reproduced, distributed, or transmitted in any form or by any means, including photocopying, recording, or other electronic or mechanical methods, without the prior written permission of the publisher, except in the case of brief quotations embodied in critical reviews and certain other noncommercial uses permitted by copyright law. For permission requests, write to the publisher, addressed "Attention: Permissions Coordinator," at the address below.

Tomiko Cobb
4002 Hwy 78 W Ste. 530-211
Snellville, GA 30039
www.publishingdreamsagency.com

Hi, my name is BJ! Welcome to my neighborhood. In my neighborhood, there are lots of important people. These people help my neighborhood in many ways.

Every morning I wake up, get dressed, eat breakfast, and walk to school. On my way to school, I pass important people called community helpers.

Want to see my neighborhood? Let's take a walk!

My first stop is Sugar Mama's Bakery. Ms. Jackie is a baker, and gives me a doughnut and a weekly allowance for taking the trash to the dumpster every day.

Twice a week, the sanitation workers come to collect the trash.

As I walk in the neighborhood, I see my new friend James! James and his dad live on a farm with goats, pigs, sheep, and cows. There is a large field of corn behind his house. His dad is a farmer.

As I am walking down the street, Mr. Davis, the grocery store manager, is opening the store. We go there to buy groceries and household items.

Around the corner is the fire station. Firefighters rescue people from fires and accidents.

As I pass the neighborhood clinic, I remembered when I was younger, I went there for a health exam for school. Doctors and nurses treat you when you are sick and help you live a healthy lifestyle.

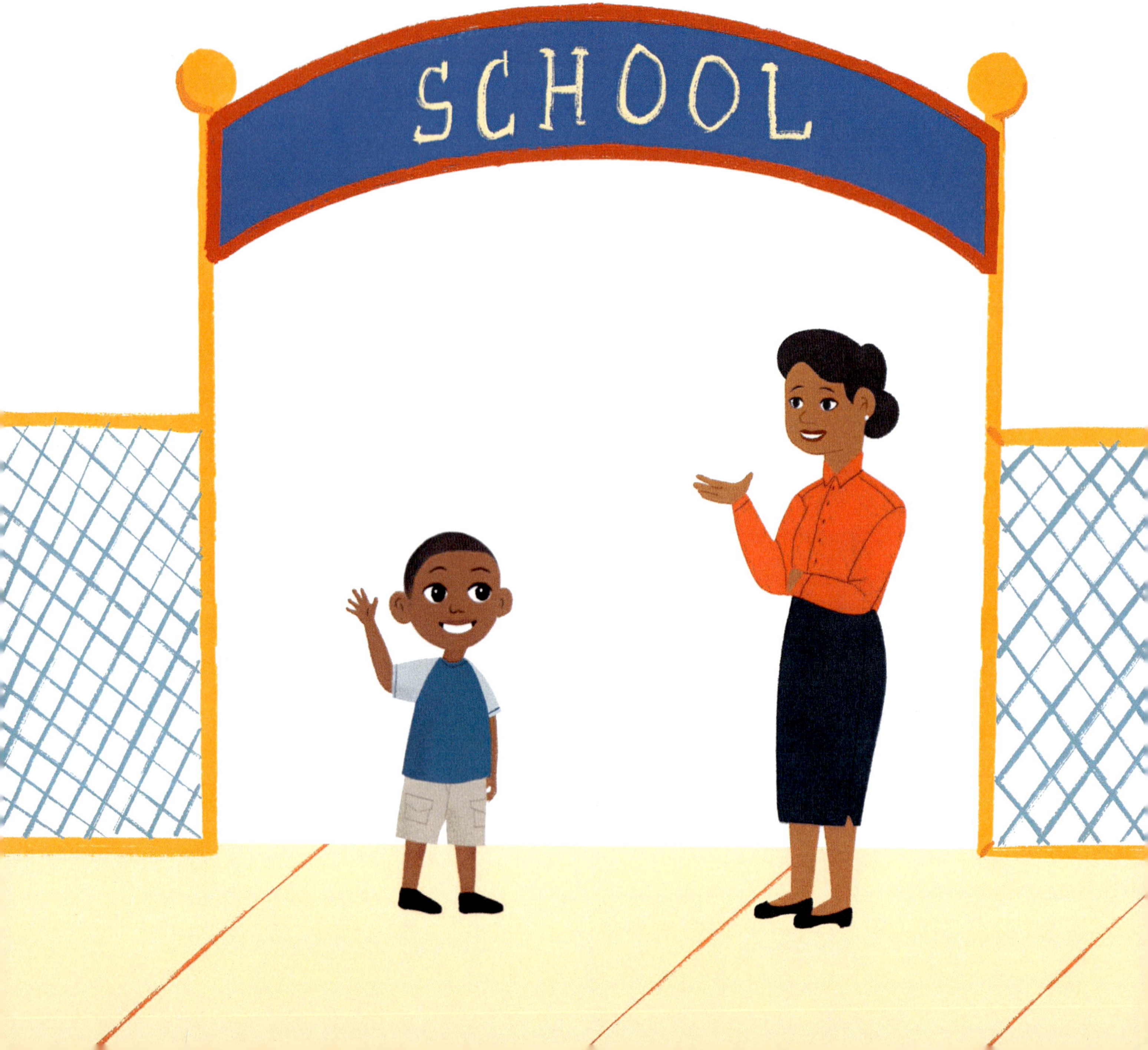
SCHOOL

Finally, Mrs. Nelson is waiting in front of the school. "Good morning, BJ" she says. "Good morning Mrs. Nelson" I reply.

As I sit in our class and listen to Mrs. Nelson teach, I glanced out the window at my neighborhood and smiled...

I love my neighborhood and all the community helpers that make it a better place!

GUIDING QUESTIONS:

What is a community helper? What makes a community?

What are some names of community helpers in your neighborhood?

What kind of uniform does your community helper wear?

What kind of tools does your community helper use?

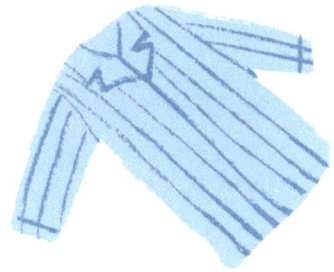

What kind of community helpers can be found in a rural community but not necessarily an urban community?

What are the duties, uniforms, responsibilities, place of businesses and tools community helpers use?

How do community helpers make communities better places to live in?

What is an occupation?

Made in the USA
Columbia, SC
03 December 2022